SPLIT-IMAGE FOCUS
The Poetry of Lila Swift Monell

Split-Image

FOCUS

The Poetry of

LILA SWIFT MONELL

Foreword by Dorothy A. Brown • *Preface by* Beverly Quint
Designed by Kathleen Valentine

Parlez-Moi Press • Gloucester, Massachusetts

ISBN: 0-9657717-1-7
For further information contact:
      Parlez-Moi Press
      Gloucester, Massachusetts 01930
      www.parlezmoipress.com

Cover photography:
Martha Graham by Lila Swift Monell, digital collage by Kathleen Valentine

Title page photography:
Auntie Also by Lila Swift Monell

Line drawings accompanying individual poems by Lila Swift Monell

Book design by Kathleen Valentine, www.valentine-design.com

Printed by PrintSmart, New Bedford, Massachusetts, USA

Parlez-Moi Press
an imprint of Mojo Publishing
Gloucester, Massachusetts USA
www.parlezmoipress.com

Preface

No sooner did I embrace the honor of writing a preface to Lila Swift Monell's book of poetry then I asked myself two questions.

First: Which poems shall I include; how can I not include all the poems spanning the past, very productive, twelve years?

Then: Shall I attempt to change Lila's spelling and punctuation, to make them more conventionally conforming; or, shall I see their originality as part of her self presentation, a stylistic representation of that "split-image focus" that defines her work and gives the book its title? (See "Elegy to Alphonse".)

A photography teacher once said of Lila's pictures that Lila saw things that were barely there. So, too, in the word pictures of her poems, she sees not just with eye focus, but with skin apprehension, with, yes, ears, tongue, webbed feet. She is both inside and outside her subjects and inside her envisioning those subjects and of herself seeing the envisioning. She is the goose and the bumblebee and the bereft wife coming home to the funeral bouquets. Hers is a unique vision, spoken in a soft...at times, halting... voice that grows in power the more we read her.

So I decided to include the complete poems of the last decade and let them suggest the vision that informs her work. If I am arbitrary, I accept the designation. I have also decided to let, with the barest minimal alterations, Lila's original spellings and punctuations stand as they are. (I think of Hart Crane and the Greenberg manuscripts; more deliberately, of ee cummings.) The structure of the poems does not depend, with this poet, on strict adherence to any linguistic map.

Lila's journey is not one of single level narrative. Her split-image focus takes us into many realms of experience simultaneously. She is the goose alive , the goose dead, the attacking dog, the uncomprehending daughter, the grieving mother and the ocean which confronts it all. Isn't that what poetry is about?

As writers we are constantly being told, "Don't tell it; show it." Lila shows it and, for that reason, does not always say it in conventional wordspeak. (See the repeated last word of her "Pictures in a Photograph Album#2.) Her vision is freefloating and we are drawn in and pulsate with it. We look down at our perfect peel of snakeskin, at our webbed feet. This is the mark of a poet.

It is Lila's mark. Here, in chronological order, welcome to the world of her poetry.

- Beverly Quint
Rockport, Massachusetts
July 2004

Foreword

What is there about Cape Ann? We seem to have more than our share of artists, writers, poets and other creative types. Some start here and stay and some come here and stay, some start here and leave and some just visit, but Cape Ann is inextricably bound to their work.

I can't remember when I didn't know Lila; first as the adorable little sister of my Swift friends and then as a close friend when she and her husband settled permanently in Gloucester to raise a family.

Of course I knew she was creative - one of her woodcuts hangs over my mantle. Of course I knew she had a special way of seeing things when I was privileged to see her photographs. But I didn't know she was a poet! Perhaps I should have known someone as private and as sensitive as Lila would write - but I didn't. I knew that this was her world - our rocks and shoreline, and our very special flora and fauna.

We all know who to call when there is a sick bird or animal.

> - Dorothy A. Brown
> Gloucester, Massachusetts
> July 2004

Split-Image
FOCUS

Talking to a Leaf

#1

Entrance my heart.
I dare you.
Just step
    inside
    and
    see
    the
      carnage there...

Behind my back
the cat is climbing a tree
I itch no more

Breaking the sunrise
    a
      crow
  rides
  insults
  across the sky.

I dream of mirages
of fish flake
happenings,
of hapless massages
to a failing, flailing heart-

                                    - break.

Upon Emptying My Pockets
  drills,bits,counter-
  sinks and routers

  There is a round
  smooth shank of steel
  all innocence and allure
  formed by man
  for participation
  where when it joins
  its master
  and there inserted
  it becomes
  a swirling streak of heat
  with grooves that bite
  as metals meet
  and shining curls
  are torn away
  and flung
  to split my eye-balls
    into a myriad
      of tears.

PICTURES IN A PHOTOGRAPH ALBUM #1

Like loose pictures
in a photograph album
you have come upon
my many loves.

Meandering through rough walls
burdened by
indiscriminate vines
lie across the page;
their ordered bones,
each still and adamant rock,
drop a perfect edge
along the fields.

Quiet afternoons
are held, lit
in fading expectation
as people draw together,
whisper together,
grateful secrets shared,
as gray shapes gather
against small houses
that drift
into the arpeggio
of vanishing hills.

A mother frowning
in endless stillness

holds away from her
a smiling infant
who searches forever
those silent eyes.

Black ribbons tear
at the heart of paper pages
as turning rips
at the heart of memory.

This is a poem to My Daughter, Francena

Turning her head to love,
To you, to me, to whoever looks at her.
Impatient hips and bosoms
Awake the day.
Were impetuous the needs
That pull her, so do they bind,
So do they tumble, roil,
(vulnerable as a rabbits pulse)
Blue-veined they rush her headlong,
heart-lung, lunging
Into longing
For a forever feeling.
The ache of sunrise
Adorns her yellow hair.
Did I give you this...
Did I give you enough...

DOCKING PUPPY-DOG TAILS

The Audience No. 1
Caterpillars

The sharp and acrid smell
of juniper branches
prick and weep my palms
while myriads of sticky
ravengers sing Hosannas
to the "snip" "snip".
The swaying caterpillars
watch,
blue-green in a blue-green hedge.

DOCKING PUPPY-DOG TAILS

The Audience No. 2

The big big fingers
of my father's hands
grasp gently, barely touching,
entwine, the blazing
bend of scissors.
       Hold back,
       breathing,
with hovering shoulders
my parent whisper,
glance,
       and then cradle
       warm black bodies.
Unbearable shining curls
wind around my fingers
while golden acacia balls
blossom against the sun.
       All hidden
       I, in the shade
       with locks of puppy silk
       surrounding;
          a bloodless nubbin, inert,
          lies by my toes,
          cool and still.

PEOPLE - who drink; frequent bars,
vote against prohibition

PEAPLE - who fear; join the Klu-Klux-Klan
with B.O. buy Lifeboy,
believe adds
are naive

PEEPLE - with feathers;
read myths,
buy insurance,
loose out
anyway.

PPLE like velcro; scream
when they are
pulled apart.

PLE is what the moon
does to
lemmings.

L is luminescence
weeping.

Starlings

I don't know where I am.
Perhaps I am in Peoria, Illinois. I am
a traveling salesman. All shoe-salesmen
have been in Peoria, Ill. It fits.
Across the flat land, under a low
sky the travelling salesmen gather.
Through the cornstalks
lizard legged
they walk.
Like Grouch Marx, intent, distracted,
stridefull,
eyes akimbo,
yellow slender legs
(tucked up on frosty mornings)
doing busy-work.
Black cloaks becoming
startling iridescence;
spots and spots and spots.
Open beaks searching,
"Who will buy my shoes
Who will buy my shoes..."
Find the right box
pull them all down
open them all up
leave tissue paper
across the land
strewn against the fences
flattened
torn

migrating south.
Great sighs of grey
heave and roll
across the sky.
The soft whisper of diminution
silken, liquid,
narrows
into
osmotic communication.
"Who will buy my shoes..."
explosions over the distant mountains
"Who will open the boxes..."
spilling down
"Who will loose the tissue..."

Shade Trees at Evening

Fingers reaching clouds,
tips touching
the round of sky
caress the passage of day.
The heat,
the breeze calling,
cooling;
the night domes,
arches, turns,
closing the folded palm.
Cats-cradle of gossamer webs
holds the dream of legend leaves,
which bending trunks
unburden.

LIGHT

Like a child led.
Led because it opened
wide its innocence; fearless, rushing
to take my hand
where others would demure,
blanketed in caution.
      and come upon -into-
      the breath-taking
      shower of stars spilling
      through the hair
      down the forehead
      caught in an eyelash
      so the world kaleidoscopes
      for a second,
      bounces off shoulders
      reaching for and caught
      squeezed into flat
      glistening finger-prints
      tracing thighs to the floor,
      surrounding us
      in pools of reflected light.
      Shimmering, love-shot
      from the body,
      gifting the air
      with a galaxy of grace.

PHOTOGRAPH OF DEAD BIRD

The Swallow

Came to me briefly and stayed,
Passed out of itself
and in it's death stayed,
disencumbered.
In its shimmering grayness
I saw a wraith,
silver-splintering,
fleeing into shadow beings.

Dancing free,
in and out
of light and focus
into radiances'
splendid promise
of decay.

I Dream Of

The city in my skin,
tall buildings grow
up through my body
and my head.

I am the skyscrapers
holder of girders
     and walls
I am the evening
     and the lights
I am the thrall of brightness
    of brightness

I am the beholder
you are there
and as the night yields
those light light
defining the emptiness
the stillness

until the rains rush down
       then wait
patient bunching avenues
         pause
awash with brilliance.

I am the lives that slide
over and down the hills
into diminishing
vistas and edges
slipping away
over the worn and secret
carpets and wordless walls

while outside is all life
honkings, door-slams, calls
excited splashes
paint sidewalks in sudden light
silver for your feet to hold
windows beckon as you pass
expect the faces of glass
that suck you in
then give you back
the night renewed
impatient for the next.

I watch
shadows race upon you
from behind
then swiftly pass
exploding into the darkness
beyond.

Beyond,
the foot-steps.
I am the short brief
echo of each.
Beyond,
the eagerness,
the weight,
the footsteps
like heart beats.
      The lightness
      and splashes...

#2

Recollections Upon Awakening

      Dreams that sleep-walk
      Slide across the sea
      And under the doors,
         To finger up the walls.

SPIDER ON FRIDAY

(The *or* Visit)

Out of the invisible
Rivers of the air
Exploded into the eye
The infinitesimal
       Dot.
Soaring its heart out,
Suspending,
Dropping its perfect
       Blue
100 stories down.
Legs fragmented,
Across the mountains
Of my knuckles
It canters
Only to disappear.

Untitled

As leaves in a wind
splatter the sunlight
into hidden places

so lifting your face
unbinds the flute
where skeins of song
beneath my skin
now dapple.

What Makes Me Hot

        The electric blanket on my
bed makes me hot.
        I turn it on when
I first start to bed,
before I brush my teeth,
turn out the lights
and skin off my outer
layer of cloths.
        Then I slip between
the covers. It's warm,
but somehow not enough.
I can't convince myself
it's body heat,
and body is what I need.

        Invite the dear old
shaggy, warm and loving
family dog onto my bed;
she's been dead, yes,
quite a few years now.
        She's been told, too,
        not to get up
        upon the bed.

So, how do you convince
a dead dog, dear dog,
to do your bidding ?
        You whisper,
        pat the covers,
        cajole,
        "Hurry now".

Remember where
she most likes
that tender rub.
        And up
        yes, one paw,
        and then another
        and then that weight,
        that over-weight mass
        of longing to please
        is up,
        down at your feet
        then at your side.

        One great tremulous
                        moment
        she stands,
        so full
        so full of love
        she must lie down quick.
        Quick before it's noticed
        she's on the bed and banished.
        Lie down and vanish.
        Blissful to be there,
        invisible,
        heart-pounding.

Body heat is what
you want.
Slide your hand under,
heart under.
Pounding with the weight
of it
the heat of it.

Late Nights
In Calexico

or
Love Song
To A-Cup-A

You were my balm, my
        chicken soup
zippering through my
            nostrils
dribbling down my
          chin
succor in that
     sinking night.

You are my sweet and
     vaulting yawn.
a whistle-wart
     upon my thoughts.

Like Gulliver held down
by the Lilliputians,
so my mother,
scissored and thimbled,
mouth bristling with pins
--pins both of steel
and some never
touched sorrow--
locks me to her,
binding in muslin
the mysteries and privacies
of my awakening landscapes.

You seem to be on such
Good terms with "time".
As if time were an ally,
You have tamed him,
Molded him to your needs.
So, placing your arm
In his,
"Yes, shall
We now dance ..."

A few days ago I celebrated and
brought home two "fire millipedes",
beautiful sparkling creatures. They
crawled and clung and fed and fed,
crapped too. Then suddenly disaster,
1/2 of one became paralyzed then he broke
in two and died. The other soon bent
and slowly ceased to work...

Elegy to Two Millipedes

Brave colors
red and black,
your million zillion
legs of scarlet,
flashing, pair
an undulating unison.
Prayers in grave
adulating grace
to detritus, enfolding,
you would
to your million breasts
had not
heartbeats
exploded
that million times
at once
and still.

An Elegy to Martha Graham*

Whose Waggish Wopish
Eyes pop at me, traced
In black and sable-brushed
Delineation
For some Wondrous
Celebration.

Whose Polka-dotted
       Flanks, dance, ignite
In gaudy pursuit.

       Whose strut-step-
       aside to ever
       -titillating-
       trips of unexpected
           angles

          REJOICE

In thunder-toes
You grasp my breath
And tramp upon my
       sensibilities
(those tidy rows of roses)

Whose is it to

          REJOICE

For how I weep
When you have vanished
And through the woods
I follow
And only dust
      Rises
And only one
Feather
Drifting down
Tells
      me
          all.

* *Ed. Note: Martha Graham was the name of a guinea hen.*

More Elegies to Be

The moon calls out
High by the guinea
                    fowl roost
Below the leaves stir.

Calling each other
The moon and the guinea
                    fowl
Are heard below.

Listening below
To guinea fowl whispering
The moon hears
        it all.

As guinea fowl
Whisper together
Call to each other
Call out
        the moon slips down.

i am

      as removed as
      a snake in dream
            still tongued
            and blind

Upside Down

The tortoises legs wave
About. Like miniature
Elephant feet they
Wave in their "onesy" skin
From inside his shell
Searching the clouds
For sand.

The moon comes around
more often now,
neccho wafered,
sassafras lipped;
tightly this communion
bowl is stretched to tilt
into the passing day.

Walking at Night

Glass is a hole
night looks through, is
waiting, waiting.

Streets wet
with autumn leaves
echo in silver
against the arc
of night.

Rows and rows and
rows of windows
stern as preachers
in a book
neat as sparrow
on a wire.

Teeth are so dry
touching
the tight skin Persimmon
is salt, bitter, and
sudden.

His raised arms measure
            his grief against
                      a cloud
a pool of water

An empty house
smooth nights embed
into each
echo corner
so utterly bare, so
utterly far away
in wood and wall
and arms and empty, smooth
this body house.

Holiday

He left me
vast and awkward
a lump upon
the bed, silent
as an ailing
camel must be
in the wastes of
some far desert,
looming and still,
an immense and
single grain of
sand.

posted inside the deep freeze

ELEGY TO ALPHONSE

Would you like to meet

Here's Alphonse, Number One
after Martha Graham.
He was a rather
stand-offish bird, until
it happened, until Martha Graham was done in.
Then things changed.
Someone had to change.

He and his father, Mic-Mac,
had to fight it out.
It was more a bluff-out.

Then everyone knew.

Back and forth he danced
and ordered;
everyone,
even every feather knew.
Like a split-image focus
each sharpened his alignment
with the other.

How he danced,
those few days.
Till circumstance over-took,
over-did, over-reached
itself, forever.

Now, no one runs things, there is a certain fatalistic
orderliness...
But the charge is out.

Something will come along.
They'll wait.
They're waiting,
now...

night birds lift
the dawn
then leave

blue drops into place
beneath
the far mountain

memories mark the grass
as hollow noon
wells colossal
endless

shhhh

a crease of fear
muffles, darkens
moves across the air
staining into night.

TERRARIUM

He moves a dance of
exquisite singleness,
pungent, iridescent.
Cymbals break the air
that only dust mots stir.

Weaving through and back upon himself
liquid as thought,
a razor silent song
of vanishing umbers.

Notes drifting down
from where he once was
and is perhaps, now.

A quiver of green.
Green on green on green
through tonal shadows
sibilant with stealth,
stretching
limber needled limbs.

> to stay
> to stop
>   to tremble

Do you feel the earth rock
forest tilt, lean sideways
spilling coils of gold,
only to snap back again,
tearing at the clouds...

        To tremble?

It is only a snake
in this terrarium
leaving his small tree.

Maybe...

'Maybe' is such a silent word
a non-thought
      non felt
      flailing
      empty
      endless
          word.

It scrapes clean the bowl
of any salt
and shouting

it mocks our silences
makes mere velvet
of our fear
numbing in a second
our chances for breath.

Fingerless and deaf
it wraps its scarf
around our heads
and presses us on.....

Pictures In A Photograph Album #2

In faded isolation,
arbiter of curt generations,
a single house stands,
it's sepia separateness
shuttered and buttressed
against the threat
of outside worlds
          sits askew the page.

Figures drawn together
on a hill,
like magnets or savage ants
-grains of diverse sands-
enrage together.
With talking hats
indifferent umbrellas stab
cacophony at funerals.
Blue gossip streaming
from the page asks for blood
          as blood runs thin,
          runs out.

A mother holds away from her
a smiling baby.
One hand supports
the eager neck and head.

Her fingers question
lightly on his arm
      who asks for love,
      as love runs out.

Wood and black
and brass-cornered,
now the steamer trunk
lies agape,
spilling
lace and porcelain
faucet handles,
hot and cold
and cold.

MR. SILENT, THE SNAKE
or Out of the Mouths of Snakes Come Snakes

Have you ever
taken off a glove
with one hand?

Think about it.
Feel about it.

Do you pull each finger back; and with it follows warm and snug
the glove!

So when Mr. Silent Snake
feels full,
feels tight
the time has
come to grow.
His belly's full
of smallish bugs,
and that is why
he feels too snug.

Mr. Silent
needs nor to grow;
to find a larger self
with which to snake in.

Therefore he sheds his skin;
his outside, scale-side;
must give way
to inside, skin-side,
fast becoming scale-side, too.

So, opening wide his mouth
as with a yawn
- a great humongous yawn -
and twisting head from
side to side,
his skin-side starts
to slip away.

The nose, the lips, are free,
the perfect eyes are
rounds of gossamer
transparency.

A tissue bonnet
drops behind
and from inside
a head appears,
all flashing eye and darting tongue,
but now, the rest:

Across a rock he rubs
his sides and curls around
another; into a plant
he loops a figure eight.

Half-way down
his graceful length
the leaves and branches
hold his skin,
this perfect peel,
behind him;
and out of it
he comes...

Fresh, and new,
and bright -
and snug no more.

Just right,
and comfortable,
and bigger, too...

SAFARDIC CLEAVER
(decorated with a horse's head)

Such stark survival
in a cleavers
fashioned iron
though
why inflict
the horse
with such a
gruesome deed.

This metal
made with infinite
devotion
weighted and devised for
        small bones
yet waiting for
        the heft
        the cry
        the arm raised

Surely
the horses
eye must roll
as skyward
he is thrust
-to never wander with the clouds-

But to suspect
that which is next
       what gash
       what crack
       as bones explode
small bird
or rabbit
or tendons in the leg of a spring lamb
-already they have shout their cry-

Ah horse head
you seem serene
but I would guess
inside
"The Guernica"
       rages
as each time
your cleaver handles' warmed
by man.

LAPEYRE STAIR

I contemplate
your unique stair
and am reminded of:

The early
slow-motion
pictures
of a galloping horse.
That precise and
liquid jointed
bone flexed step,
as grave and intricate
as any dance
a dead bird executes
tumbling from the sky.

That step I never could
quite learn
at dancing school.
Being shy of stumbling
and sweaty palms,
I never learned
to try
and so I left.

Or shaking hands
at graduation;
first one hand forward, shake,
back, and then the other, diploma

Or with the same
self-conscious cadence
as taking of
the blood and flesh
of christ communion day.

I contemplate
myself
to see how I proceed
with each excruciating touch
and breath and care
that I be back again
at dancing school
where I never learned
to try,
and so I left.

ELEGY TO AUNTIE

It was Auntie, killed,
this time by a fox
who circled and circled,
breaking through the crust
enough to leave a shadow of
his quickening intention
his questing pant shortens
hotter
as his steps press closer.
Even a fox, I would guess,
must let his heartbeat beat louder
-inside,
blood rush redder through
the rapids of his veins-

Old lover once, Old Aunt Also,
forever morose in her unique grief
of being lost, turned down
forever, by the guinea cock, Martha Graham.

Almost as if he spurned her memory
her pull and yearn became
a rage to him.

Auntie, for years the cat brier
tangle was your most cherished place
except beneath my dining room table.

Of all the birds
you found a gentle solace
there.
You were very difficult to remove
tiptoe to one side
as I came round the other.
You forced me
on my knees many a time -
to become like you
tiptoed, serene, with a certain self assurance.
Did you want to speak
to me, under that table?
or when we stalemated inside the briers?

I think you did, I think you have,
for now I have you in my arms
what's left of you --
blood and hollow and matted feathers
headless, thank god,
but with two perfect legs.

Not to dance
but to steal around the secret floors of wood
and to quietly articulate
your footprints
in and out my heart forever.

I hold two legs,
one, still with its
twin bracelets of blue plastic.

Remember

Auntie-Also
do you remember when
you shared a nest
a nest with Tattle-Tale
a communal nest
and broodiness
grabbed you both
at once
intense and particular
you each dealt
with small bits
of branch and leaf
to set the scene
of housekeeping
some instinct told you
it was time
could be the numbers, thirty eggs
could be the daylight hours, lengthening
you both ached to fit
the fullness of the hollow
beneath the blueberry bushes
but then began the quarreling
through the afternoon
and far into the night
      whose egg is this
      that's mine
      not mine
and back and forth you bickered
as one retrieved an egg
from the other the other
slipped out one from behind
I should have known that
every creature near and far
could hear the bedroom quarrel
the last I saw
before I went to bed

was Tattle-Tale ringed
with eggs
a wreath of cobbled white
she who told me tales
of where your nests were hidden
now had the "lion's share" herself
(I could almost see her smile)
then only hours later
you, Auntie, were at the upstairs door
frightened and distraught
calling out at this chaotic night
your cry of anguish
impaling terror into the heart
of every hidden sleepless
bird around
a raccoon had heard
complaints
       the who's whose
       that's mine
       oh no you don't
and come and taken
off the nest Tattle-Tale
the layer
the body belonging to those eggs
and torn apart the process
the rhythm the drive as strong
as tides as winds
had ravaged and plundered
had taken Tattle-Tale
taken what he could to his domain
and, Auntie, you were left
left to wander dazed
and desolate
left with some broken eggs
and some whole
Mic-Mac, Alphonse, She and Her
came to those eggs left
those and you I rescued
so the wold went on
without you, Tattle-Tale
yet each passing
seems to mark deeper.

Elegy to a Guinea Hen

There certainly was mayhem
in that tree last night
-the tree- you roost in-
sharp twigs
and broken bits
of white pine branches
spread across the snow
as if some small storm
had carelessly passed through.

Bits of feather have rested
on the crystalline white ground,
drifting down in
some far-away
Viennese waltz
gliding back and forth
unawares of past or future,
to settle, in the morning sun.

Spots of blood, too
not red but stains
of luminescent rust.

Oh what were you thinking
when whatever, whoever, it was
came out of that still night and struck.

Can you contemplate death
or only fear and pain...
that's enough.
Too much for an ungainly bird,
for a trusting bird
at least as far as
trust can reach, in you.

Confusion must have ricocheted
inside your tiny skull

as your ample body
filled with pain.

Did you cry out
or were you silent
through the tearing-

Like children of the bomb
stood mute while
skin replaced over flesh
that sometimes wasn't even there,
over child-bone alone.

Did you feel
his hot breath
mixed with your hot blood...
it shows in the snow
paw prints
bird prints
mingle, skid and thrust
in a jagged duet.

Did you look over your shoulder
in search of something, someone...
wake up, if you ever dreamed...

look for this pain to stop
look for this battering to quit
        did you keep looking
        did you keep hope
until you had no head
                no you
                no hope
Now it is left
for us to have,
what there is of you.

What there was of you
will stay with us,
        your independence
        your effort
        your sincerity at being bird.

The Service

I am full of
funeral food
yet it does not help.

The church is full of
beautiful bone-structures.
Profiles that glow,
heads bowed
or held high,
have a special majesty
in church.
Why?

Why in church is
one so successful at
that individual essence-
as if there each his sorrow
becomes articulated and refined.
Is it:
here am I all whole,
full of knowledge of the joys
and anguishes of life?
Walking down the aisles
giving or taking surcease
in that perfect coat
or cadence...

Not –

How did I ever find my way here.
(Though I have been here often)

What were those things
that kept me
from closing my front door:
        the scarf,
        the newspapers on the floor,
        let last nights' dishes
        soak a little longer,
        summer is soon enough
        to paint the house --
And so I get to church.
Each step had been an
anguish of decision.
Each step, approaching a crevasse
or a discussion with an avalanche.
It took me years.

And now a minuet
of grief is playing on the walls,
dancing in the sunlight
streaming in the windows.

Only the husband - so chilled
the children - grown, or so they thought,
and many others,
experience what they never
knew was there.
  -this devastation-
Never knew was lurking,
waiting, to softly guide them
by the elbow,
had always been
with each one,
  -this devastation-
waiting to step forward,
and no one
ever told them
it was there.

RAT

I who was going to
tender that rattling watch:

the silver whiskers
pounced out of perfect
obsidian delection
quivering for
information

small fire-cracker toes
inscribe
an insatiable haste
across the snow

- this tentative
tail-trails nervous
sparrow-seekings,
language and this
rattiness bone-haste -

Back to her pulsing nest,
ravening
3-single, 4-single, five
hairs on that avid
grey scaled tail
is sharp as any scant
ear and wondrous eye.

Is she more lizard than I...
Is back to her hot nest,
tearful, fearful, driven,

wet with large windy memories
howling her urgency,
more real than any dream
I lizard, I bird, I blind
clumsy man can enter into...

I find myself started into her world,
she is only inconvenienced.

I find myself longing
for her memories, her libidinousness,
her league of endless damp continents.

Valleys of drifts of whispers
what can they tell me...
Can I sustain this
rat heat nestling, cherish
this pink lusting skin,
infinitely toe-nailed, veined, and tailed,
infinitely naked,
oblivious, satiated.

Did it take eons
to satisfy,
- so simply, swiftly, sweetly -
completely;
almost into death so sublimely.

Will she be with us,
        after me....

Spring #1

It is March,
wet with melt and change.
The foxes are screaming;
short tight shouts,
cries
that dart about the darkness
and turn the roomed and windowed
into fear and loneliness
at the looseness,
at the craven ease of desire,
at the piercing liquid night.

LOVE

The bumblebees are mating
on the porch deck
He pounds at her:
seven, eight, nine;
then backs away.

Hovering, he flies forward,
bumps her again
and again.
Get up, get up,
You lazy bitch.

She's supine, still;
head down upon
the splintery wood.

Flying he tends her,
circling; a perfect
circumference;
his relaxed, spiky legs,
hung down.

Hear the hum of
invisible wings;
and again, again.
Crawling she toes
slowly, crab-wise,
with bent, patent leather joints.

Her heavy, black legs take her;
tentative, unsure, on a meandering trail.
Then remembering;
quickly; she lifts.
She flies away;
     you bum,
     you bum.

Journal of a Victim

Hurt animals
hump around
and push their heads
to corners.
Bow down,
slow down,
      avoid the body intrusions
          of others,
      even your own
      intrudes and breaks
          the heart
      that slowly slowly
          questioning
            downhill;

      walk softly,
          sideways, (is that a shadow, lurking, seeking,
            I see no shadow now - no light)
          bent down.
          Delicately place the foot
          forward, dare the body...
This body becomes so heavy,
the head stretches forward
rhythmically, with each step,
          pulls the heaviness,
          pulls the blackness,
          blurring
          fervently trying not
          to be,
          to slowly step,
            slowly.

Lift your back, compress the pain just inside the
intricate joints of those arched bone. Pain squeezed
through, ripples the monochromed pulse of fear.

Wait, is there blue turning to lavender
              sliding into rose and light,
                lightness and morning, daybreak...
    When it comes again
    rushing through,
    weakening legs.

Bird
Bird
Bird   so frail and feathered
           and now so bent and broken
           with numb longings that never unfold
           in the corners of your roost,
           in the dust-dross of broken feathers,
           brittle sheaths, remnants,
           reminders you were once there
           in ernest.

Damaged: You are so faltering,
           slight, vacillate, are reduced,
           as gusts of anger press
           down upon the skin,
           the irresolute mind.

The determination that once stood alone,
        no longer is a part of you,
        or friend.

Damaged now;
           Kill him
           the aunt says, kill him
           the sister, the brother
           the mother pecks him to the ground.
           (not the fey uncle

who dances about in coquettish disbelief,
until he too bows his head,
cowers in the bushes,
jerks his head aside
avoiding in pantomime
that blow to you.)

The drive that
with each strike
brings blood,
that is sinister
bubble of red,
hypnotizes.

An ooze
that draws the others to it,
to stare,
cock their heads,
stab
and jab at it.

One pauses, wipes her beak
against brown leaves,
then runs again to you,
runs to whoever she can find.

(HE will run from you.
You will chase him.
Out of bounds you will push him,
past the intimate bristle
of bushes and weeds;
where the echoes of his unexpected song
slant off the walls of secure boards
to filter familiar through the trees.)

Why this blood thirst
while the chickadees call...

Damaged,
You are marked.

> See how the others
> close in,
> drawn to this disarrayed
> inevitableness.

Until:

> Back to your roost of death.
> Bow down, hide your head down,
> quelled; round captive eyes
> covered from beneath and above in ancient ashen skin,
> folds of blindness
> stare at nothing,
> press against the ground
> between your feet.

> > You understand this
> > damage,
> > You wear it on your
> > bent back.
> > Your toes scrape
> > the dry dirt already,
> > waiting.

The Train to Boston

I take the train
to Boston early
when the song of birds,
the warning whistle,
mingle,
and heedless plastic cups
with tea bags
decorate the weeds.

Assigned across
the hillside cedars'
puritanical symmetries
are cedar and stone,
while the briars' green tangles
ravage the fleeting solitude.

The disenchanted
and arranged backyards
introduce us to their lives;
their shameless joys of summers
upon summers, upon summers
reemerge from snowbanks
in a rhythmic blue.

Sudden tires stare unseeing
from those shrinking banks,
piles of nightmares heave
and stir beneath.
Wake up and stretch
your rusting arms
flex your splintered glass

to catch in the morning light
the glint and slick
of plastic and oil,
before I get to Boston.

Approaching North Station,
terminated roadways like
giant broken insects
taking large steps
out of cold graves
and incomplete copulations
witness.

Sidewalks move backwards,
body midsections rush
past reflectionless
train windows,
touchless
chill
specter-flecked.
People bent
intent to not be late
leave behind
the derelict,
the joyless,
the incurious styrofoam.

As starlings search irregular
black holes in warehouse walls,
I take the train to Boston.

The carpenter ant is
lying on his back
on my kitchen counter.
His segmented blackness arches,
his head looks across and past
his body fibrillations.

He is listening to his feet
as each explores the other,
then the vastness, threading
secrets in the air, knitting
a tapestry of dying.

With knees he pivots,
each pause becomes a portion
of an invisible design;
in thrusting he divides his world
into diminishing recollections
where harsh knowledge has nibbled
into his smooth
obsidian head.

Like a paper cut-out
of the remains of a
forest fire
he is a species prone
to disproportionate
disasters.

What a frenzy it would
be were he to stand
upon his many feet,
to gavotte and craze
and nimble the elbows
into invitations,

to ululate with toes
-that to know so well
the homey cleansing of
the eye, the leg, each other.

His articulate struggle,
a shadow spread across the sky,
is as incomprehensible
as he is,
here in my kitchen
between the crumbs.

Now he is crook'd
as if to clutch
the entire air.

He tries so hard to rise,
he tries so hard
to still himself,
his many joints and pieces,
his childhood prayers.

Love Is A Brand New Bowl

And as time passes
the bowls' perfection fills.
Stars push back the sky,
reflections stretch across
the fill of light.

Memories slide inside
in circles and sing to me
in lavender.

Enormous voids coalesce
into darkening lids
of sleeping roses
until they are no more.

    Give me back my
        glass,
          my perfect round,
   waiting to be filled
   with sunny days
   and skipping stones,
   and clouds
       that never
       grow
       but guard
       forever.

THE SEASHELL

Secure Me
Close my Lids With a Strip of Paper
Print C H I N A Across my Sight

> The word for love is hidden
> inside the shiny seashell.
> A white tab seals
> the lips of promise
> from fingernails too short to rip --
> not strong enough to pull apart.
>
> Until,
> divided
> C H I N A is
> in two forever
> giving birth to
> sudden rising splendor
> with sights
> that daze
> the pump full the heart
> that dragged behind.
>
> My eyeballs stream red
> and blue seaweed flowers
> straining the liquid
> with gaudy dreams,
> boundless in the waters
> of the kitchen tumbler.
>
> My chin rests on a crocheted doily.
> My breath
> clouds the glass.
>   With my finger
> I trace the words:
> G O D and C A T
> and B A L L
>   across the sky.

Conversations with Beverly

The Common Egret flies thoughtfully
His long frail legs trail low behind,
a lure,
to speculate
in stills of watery
green privacies, where
delicate reflections
behold themselves
in dialogue.

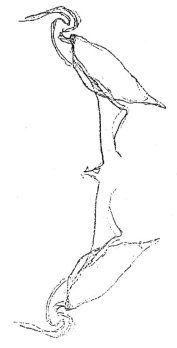

Rabbit Changes

There is something
incorrect about
a rabbit walking
down a road.
Is it the length
of his legs...
or that he,
being a rabbit, is
actually capable
of putting down one foot
in front of the other...
or is it that he moves so finely;
walks with all the time in the world...

> No fox,
> or shadows edge,
> no blade of grass,
> no vision of ancient endless plains,
> > no beckoning,
> > > to distract.

THE SERVICE #2

The priest is making vinaigrette dressing.
He speaks of sacrifice and offerings,

I think of Mayan rituals and altars,
of dripping blood from
bone pierced tongues
that speak their messages
to Gods as mighty.

and then he settles down
to serious brunch,
(the crunch, the gulp)
the corner of the
pristine white napkin
daubs at tight pursed lips,
then presses round the glass
and makes the crystal sing.

I think of rough stone goblets
soaked in the tears and sweat
of public fears,
leaden with whispers
of private agony
as shouts of play and pain
echo overhead
in the royal courts of death.

Incantations
out of wooden mouth,
disembodied
chants,

inflectionless,
filling the air
with jack-straw words,
immaculate hands
pantomime.

The congregation kneels.

The dead is full of wit and humor;
listening in to each
our private thoughts
she sheds a tear for neighbors,
for progeny that weep;
she loves,
loves the wise men who remember
and eulogize,
who dare to challenge
her yet.

I think of many priests,
I think of yesterday,
I think that that
is no time to die.

A half begotten moon
lifts reluctantly.

A yellow torpor
pulls its incomplete
edge away from
other shades.

The leaves move
in unease.
Trying not to run
to one another
they rush together,
brush up against
my breath
in unbelieving
      foreboding.

Have you never seen
true mid-night blue,
the inkstain soil
      that seeps down
      into bones
      of despair,
and a sad moon
not beseeching,
just being there.

Summer Tears

Is it so long
since you hid.
Is it so long
since then...

My thoughts stretch
around...

My heart, like water
bubbling up
uncontrollably
from a broken
faucet head,
slackens.

I hear the high song
of the night beetle
trying to put out
the stars.

All through the night
hold your breath
with them:
love their song,
love their insistence,
love putting out
the stars one by one.

The blurring song
of wings drives
all else out.

I lie down
under songs.
Wrapped in water
I watch the stars die.

Driving Home
THE RAILROAD CROSSING

Close to, the diesel horn
on the commuter train
is urgent.

From behind Great Hill
flashing its purple flanks,
    - a fish caught
     in sunlight
      has as many secrets -
surprising the narrow air
with its demands,
the train disrupts the stillness.

Impatiently the
trees re-assemble,
only the occasional leaf,
buffeted, hysterical,
left behind, insists,
     next time,
     next time.

SWINSON FARM REVISITED

The juniper placed outside
in the cement urn
it soon outgrew
is shagged over now.
Dry strips of peeling bark
distend a sentinel
for no one,

as if violin music
tore it apart, mimicking
the yellowed grasses
scraping in the wind,
the sumac's chartreuse
fingers groping
through the ground.

On it side
one half the urn
lies staring skyward
trying to recall
the warmth of hands that
filled it once, the terror of enclosed roots
the beigeness
the press of winter's rote.

Whose music heaved
the foundation slabs
to many angles of repose,
clapped with shadows

now and then
     and lichen...

Where once were rows
of corn and mounds
of peas and beans
the conifers and hardwoods
     have invaded
and over all the hush
of whine of summer
     the drone
     of alien vines.

PARTY

or
Wishing Not to be Late for Christmas

Eating other peoples
lox and capers,
breaking the crackers
of conversation,
loosing the syntax
as well as the sauce.

Clicking ones shoes
on tile and varnish,
despoiling the starch
in the linen vestments;
soaps of pink seashells,
hearts, and spheres
insert the voluptuous into the prim.

Then back to the glitter and surfeit
of voices, back to the
eye-level, ear-level,
mouth-level din.

The salmon laid out
is resting majestically -
full length
on parsley and wood -
waiting like us
for his bones
to be picked.
Dressed for the party
waiting like us.

TOAD AT CHRISTMAS

One December night
in the cold rain
up a run-off stream
from the down-hill street
a large toad hopped
across the road.

Jumping
as earnest as
heartbeats,
up through the
brilliance of
tar and star
twilight and moon.

Splashing in silver
his splay foot
determination.

His heaviness
lifting
miraculously
into the night.

THE TRAIN TO BOSTON III

     Winter is indifferent.
The field pass;
silent expanse of
grey imperfect snow
mapped by the undulant tunnels
of vagrant memories.

     Is it the blind moles
      rush
     invisible -
     their crystalline
      cries
     echo within ?

The tidal threads insist..
Sharply in the still air
the immense ice cracks,
tilts skywards.

     Winter is indifferent.
We are the wasteland.
Our broken backs
feed on the dry ground -
become the flotsam,
the musty castings
of dreamlessness.

GOSLINGS

Their lightness
boneless
bone flightlessness
wakes
in hues of spring.

Reckless legs
run haphazard
zig-zags
along the edge
of sunlight.

Have you held me
on an afternoon
in my yellowness,
my closed
umbrella feet
hanging, dangling,
vinyl creased.__

Suddenly
      sleeping.

Egret Returns

Once again the egret flies
and pokes around a bit
and gingerly places his toothpick legs
testing anew these colder waters.

Standing above the brackish mud
while freshlets and tidal floes
swirl silver bubbles
inches above his toes,
minnows dazzle and dart,
each his quicksilver appetite sated.

Slow to lift on whispering wings
slow to feel the spring-time urges
something shifts in his memory...
sings of coolness...

A hunger, delicate and symphonic,
ritualistic as the structure
of a feather.

Fred, The Resqued Seagull

Poor Fred,
dead Fred
not there
at least where he should be.
Not under the shed.
Fred, shed
dirt and feathers dry dusty...
No water left
in the plastic bath.
The cat food label
fish scales
the white smeared ledges
and large slow flies
are all that's left.

Reminders that Fred was here,
dead Fred now
and gone,
dead leaves and things forgotten
wood
and brick
a ratty grey feather.

The flash of pink on a delicate leg,
the tentative eye, the quickness,
the distrust of being,
of memory,
the questions,
the deadness of
goneness, of not,
of leaves,
of dry,
dry, dust.

Rose, I am sorry.

- he opened the file
and pulled a sheet of paper from it.
" This is you, this is about you. "
Then another man pulled another paper
from a file - " this is you " then another
and another and another
until the whole ocean was alive
with the smooth glide of the opening files,
the glints of riffling papers created
a million bright waves, and the
slide and glide and the smooth slosh
like a great whale rolling in the
sea and the water rushing from off
his back as he mammothly rolls and rolls
in the soft sea and the papers'
edges smoothly flick over and the
water runs and runs, down and
silver and deep and deeper and
you are down and down
and deeper and gone so far
over and down and the drawer
slides shut with long low
swishes leaving brushing falling away
water away until it closes
and clicks -

Passing of an Old Goose

Sing-Sing, dear goose,
why can't I write
about your death, about your life,
your life goes back so long.

My daughter, Francena, grown up now,
thinks she was sixteen
when you first climbed upon her lap.
She was sunning herself in a beach chair
and loved you at that moment,
adored you, felt your love for her
flow through your hot webbed feet
into her thighs.
You both had adolescent surges
of unbearable feelings.
Not knowing what to do with them
you let them flow,
you wallowed in them there in the warm sun
until the beach chair pinched your legs
and Sing-Sings' weight and balance toppled
her to the ground.

I thought of this as we walked down the path,
you carrying the heavy blue plastic bag
from which to place her in the ocean.

We sat on the warm poppels,
wet and silver from the ebbing tide.
First of November, fog,
the fog-horns were your knell, old goose,
the water splashed rhythmically
as afternoons pearly light encased us.

The waves searched for
the center of your weight
to lift you with the strands of seaweed,
to rock you loose,
to float you lightly,
gently, softly out to sea.
No longer heavy with the burden of age
that made you lurch and waddle
side to side in pendulous steps
across the lawn.

Floating almost, you jerked a little,
straining as a stone caught you
against the pull of the tide.
Your ungainly angled head
and neck, broken, move gracefully now,
full of languorous surrender,
lightness,
beinglessness.

I wanted to sit there forever with you,
rinsed of all fears,
dissolved.
Francena would not let me.
Is she too young to need the solace
of recognizing grief...

You were killed by a dog
whose startling eyes were like
the reflections of a pale blue sky,
two blazing cerulean holes
in his violent head.

God, I miss you,
you were an every-day experience.
You touched me with your need.
I could respond to this, gratify you.
It only took the calling of your name,
a handful of corn,
a soft gaze between us
for less than three seconds.

THE WRONG DAY

Whatever I do,
seems to be
misinformed
or want
mislaid:
The only tree left standing
after a blight.
The shrew (darting blind
across the open field)
whose next meal's escaped,
which is suddenly
and forever this meal,
this hunger,
this metabolism screaming.
I merely sit,
My skin searches the loneliness
adjusting to the pitch of light,
the insect disharmonies,
the small pale bird calls.
It is a shadowless day and
I can barely touch the edge of errors
or find the start
of my beginning.

A great blue heron
flies across the yellow marsh
the black tips of his wings
lifting and lowering
until pausing just above the grasses
he swings his legs forward beneath him
and drops onto the mud.
A marsh-hawk veers out of the sky
into a tree.
He perches and flicks his tail,
and resettles his wings
tucking and retucking them nervously,
like an old lady adjusting her
handkerchief in her sleeve,
a tight cadence of energy contained.
A crow flies into the tree
settling above the hawk.
Rocking up and down he caws
shrilling again and again,
scolding, warning ;
a black bird-seer
shattering the air with his cries,
cacophonous, oracular.

CROW IN SPRING #2

Crows
have built their nest
in a white pine
outside my kitchen window.

The pine is old, short,
stunted by the north-east winds.
I knew it years
before we cleared the brush
and built our house.
Indigenous.
Indigenous made us care
to save it
worry when the needles
yellowed, fell
softening footsteps on the driveway.

From where I stand
at the kitchen sink
and when the wind
moves the branches
I see her head
above the nest.
I see it often.
The glistening still black oval
as she faced out, away from me.

How surprising to see her there
every day when I look;

glimpsed through the uncertain shadows
where drops of pitch reflect the sun
and pale new cones enlarge, blue-green.

How surprising this crow so fixed
to her task, so predictable, motionless.
Has she placed another on her nest
to fool me...

She's slipped out of her crowishness
... for now
given her impetuous deeds,
her heckling screeches veering high
and delirious in the sky,
her head-dipping throaty-voiced
whispering, mad desires.

Do you remember peeling the bitter skin off the spotted salamander...
the trill of a bumble-bee
between your beak...

Bees

carpenter bees are
stumbling out of
their perfectly round
drill holes.

on barbed feet
they step across
the hard ground
and step again

into halos
of indecision
they circle and hum

unsure if this
is the right world.

Stonehenge at Drumlin Road

Behind the circle of stones
a black cat sits,
still as any single pebble
      at the bottom of a water quarry,
      staring at the bent
      dried grasses
      where the mouse
      has disappeared.

      Silent as an unwound clock
      and stark against the unkempt
      winter-strawed field
      he waits...

      Mum as ice
      the mouse.

GRACKLES ON MOTHER'S DAY
for Beverly Q.

The color is unrelenting,
stark, a folly in its blackness,
except in the sun
when grackles dazzle.
Rude iridescences
of light and song
they ripple languidly.

Like children in black witches garbs
they spread and open up their cloaks of wings
and shoot a yellow gimlet eye at you.
Watch out, watch out, they cry,
and fill the emptiness of air
in thrill and tremble.

Black as night
with beaks pointed at the sky
they blaspheme the blue.
Turn your head,
hold your breath,
then freeze
upwards
still as stone.

Condolences

The flowers arrive;
Delivered to us
From many places:
      Far away;
      Across the street;
      Someone's backyard;
Exotic blooms;
Lush colors:
      Pink and yellows,
      Scarlets, blue and lavenders.
How removed I feel
From all this brilliance,
From such a show of raucous colors.

They're meant to be
Talking to us,
Telling us, "It's all right
The pain will go away".

Around the room they're
Placed, arranged, deliberately,
As orderly bouquets, an
Equi-distance from one another.

So, as one walks about his home,
We cross their radar;
Messages that zap.
Us through the heart.

They're here to help us
                not forget;
To go about our chores,
To put one foot
Before the other;
To remind us that now
The front door opens
Into a different house.

Lila Swift Monell grew up in Pasadena, California, the youngest among three sisters and one brother. Yearly her family made the cross country trip to her maternal grandfather's estate on Eastern Point in Gloucester, where her love of rocks, ocean, and the wildlife in which they abounded were a lifelong influence.

Besides a marriage of fifty-two years to noted North Shore architect, Donald Monell, Lila mothered four children: three sons and a daughter. She is also, twice, a grandmother. Lila's involvement in The Arts includes, besides writing poetry, designing and manufacturing furniture, and creating works of graphic art, outstandingly, photography. Perhaps resonating with her maiden name, Swift, Lila is widely known on the North Shore of Massachusetts as "The Bird Lady", a sanctuary of last resort for injured birds and other wild woods and shore creatures.